AF585206

QUEENSLAND

Linsie Tan

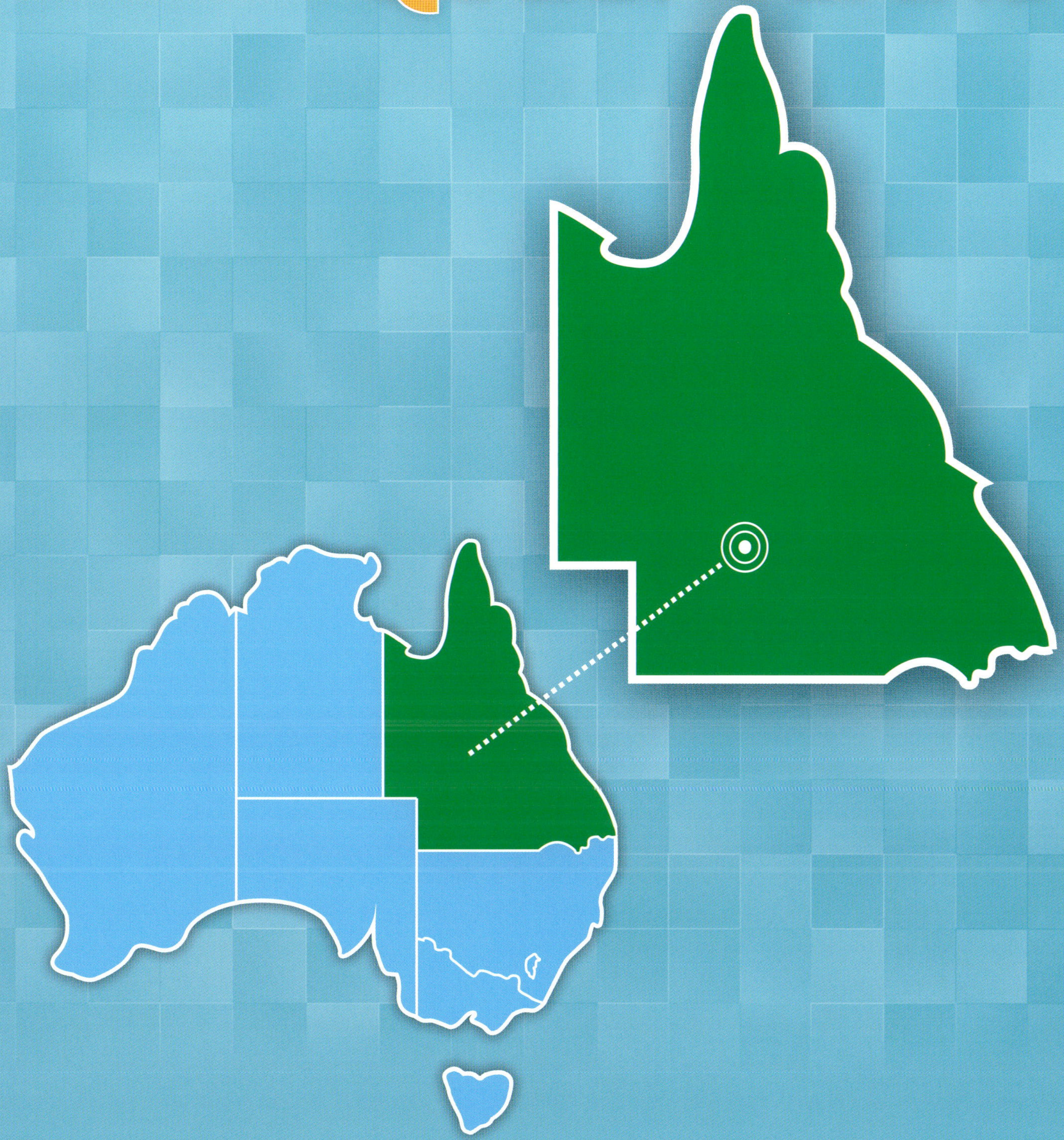

Redback Publishing
PO Box 357 Frenchs Forest NSW 2086
Australia

ISBN 978-0-9946247-3-4

First published 2017
Reprinted 2018

Author: Linsie Tan
Editor: Jane Hinchey
Original illustrations © Redback Publishing 2017
Originated by Redback Publishing
Printed and bound in China by Leo Paper

Acknowledgements
We would like to thank the following for permission to reproduce photographs: State Library of Queensland, Dixson Galleries, Mitchell Library, State Library of New South Wales, National Library of Australia, Oliver Foerstner / Shutterstock.com, ChameleonsEye / Shutterstock.com, neftali / Shutterstock.com, Tony Bowler / Shutterstock.com, carrie-nelson / Shutterstock.com, Tinseltown / Shutterstock.com, www.dfat.gov.au, Joost Evers, Jason Pini, Squiresy92 and Ravenspear82.

Every effort has been made to contact copyright holders of any material reproduced in this book. Any omissions will be rectified in subsequent printings if notice is given to the publisher.

Cataloguing-in-Publication details are available from the National Library of Australia

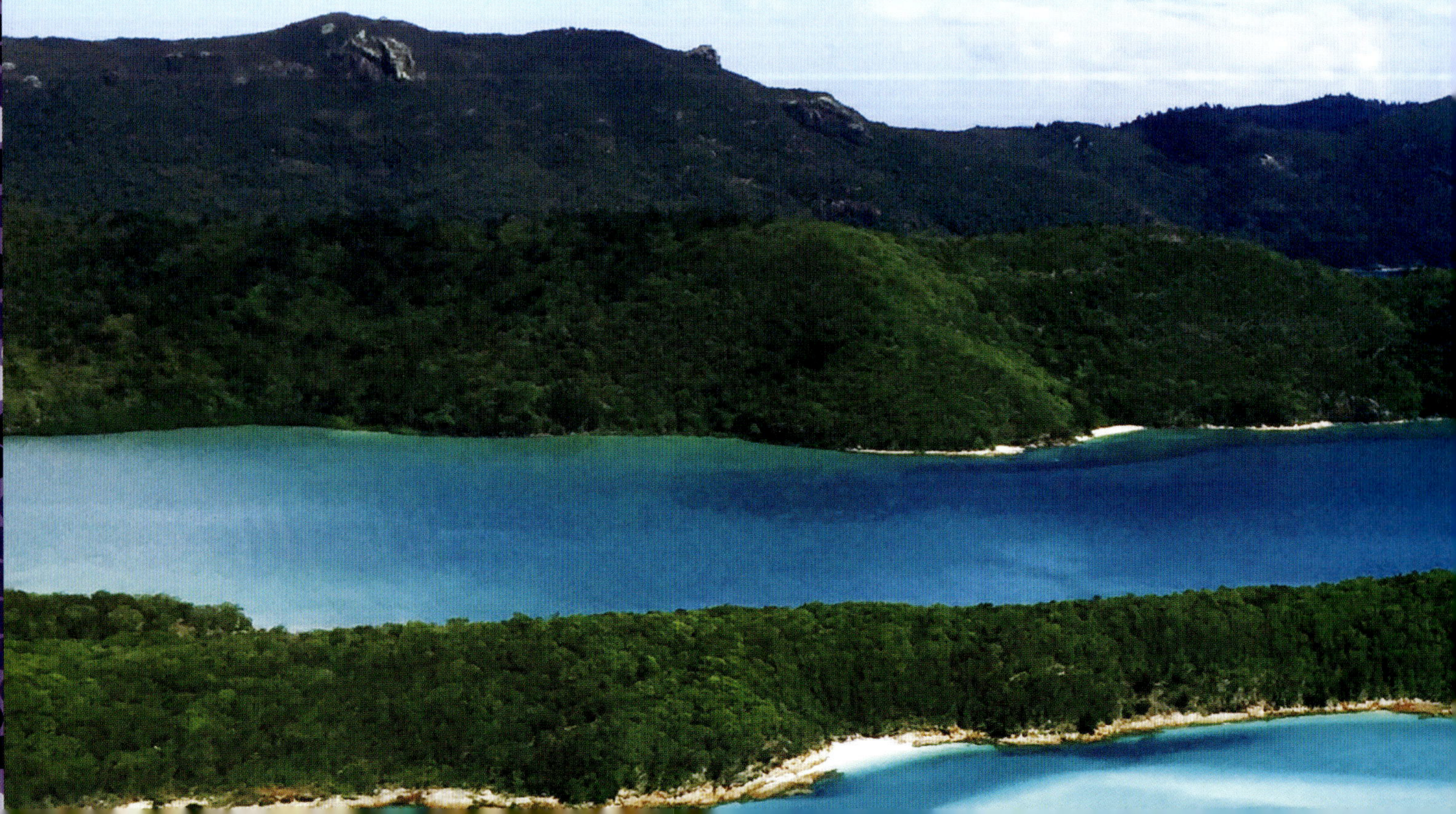

CONTENTS

Some words are shown in red, **like this**.
You can find out what they mean by looking in the glossary.

Geography of Queensland

Queensland is the second largest state of Australia. The capital city is Brisbane on the Brisbane River. The nearest country is Papua New Guinea to the north across the Torres Strait.

The Great Barrier Reef

This coral reef extends for 2,300 kilometres along Queensland's coast. It contains the world's largest range of corals and is treasured for its ecological diversity.

Mountains

The Great Dividing Range runs the whole length of Queensland. It separates the coastal lowlands and hills from the plains to the west. The highest mountain is Mount Bartle Frere at 1,622 metres high, near Cairns.

Gulf of Carpentaria

This large marine area has extensive salt flats. Cape York Peninsula is the most northern point of the Australian mainland.

The Northwest Uplands

This vast area is rich in minerals. The copper, silver, lead and zinc ores mined at Mount Isa have provided important sources of income for the Queensland economy.

FAST FACTS

The LONGEST rivers in Queensland:

- **Flinders River**
- **Mitchell River**
- **Fitzroy River**
- **Brisbane River**
- **Mary River**

Islands of Queensland

Queensland has 1,955 islands. Here are some of them:

Fraser Island - The largest sand island in the world and a popular tourist destination.

Magnetic Island - Named by Captain James Cook in 1770.

Thursday Island - The governing centre for a group of islands in the Torres Strait.

Whitsunday Islands - These are part of the Great Barrier Reef area and are popular for their tourist resorts.

Hinchinbrook Island - The largest island in the Great Barrier Reef area.

Deserts

The deserts in Queensland are home to many plants and animals that have developed adaptations to enable them to live in extreme conditions. The following deserts are partly in Queensland:

Simpson Desert - this desert is a national park. It can only be crossed in the dry season.

Sturt Stony Desert - this is a gibber desert.

Strzelecki Desert - named after Polish explorer Pawel Edmund Strzelecki.

PREDICT THE POPULATION

Draw a graph and use it to estimate what the population will be in 2040.

YEAR	1860	1890	1920	1950	1980	2010	2040
POPULATION of QLD	28,000	392,000	751,000	1,205,000	2,388,000	4,437,000	?

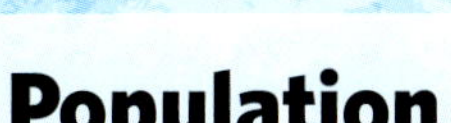

Population

There are about 4.8 million people in Queensland, with about 2.3 million living in the Brisbane area.

The next largest towns after Brisbane are Gold Coast, Sunshine Coast, Townsville and Cairns, all on the coast. In the regional areas, outside the main towns, the population is very scattered.

Climate

The climate of Queensland is temperate in the southeast around Brisbane. In the far north there is a monsoon climate and in the west the climate is very hot and dry. Tropical cyclones occur each year across the north of the state.

WORD FILE

salt flats - areas of marsh between the land and the sea

monsoon climate - a climate having two seasons, wet and dry

temperate - having a mild climate

gibber desert - desert covered in stones rather than sand

FAST FACTS

- Highest recorded temperature: 49.5 °C at Birdsville in 1972.
- Lowest recorded temperature: -10.6 °C at Stanthorpe in 1961.

Aboriginal and Torres Strait Islanders History

Aboriginal people have lived in Australia for at least 60,000 years. They developed complex societies and ways of life, and their culture depends on having strong spiritual connections to the land.

Ancient History of Queensland

Archaeologists have found items made by Aboriginal people living in the Carnarvon Ranges in central Queensland dating from 18,000 years ago. On the walls of the Kenniff Cave are pictures of hands, boomerangs, shields, and spear-throwers. The Carnarvon Ranges also feature the only ancient stencil of a whole body shape found anywhere in the world.

FAST FACTS

There may have been 120,000 to 300,000 Aboriginal people living across Queensland before colonisation by the British, but no-one knows the exact number.

The Brisbane Area

Aboriginal people had lived along the river in the Brisbane area before the convict settlement there in the 1820s, but by the 1850s there were no Aboriginal people in the centre of the settlement at Moreton Bay.

Timeline - The Torres Strait Islands

8.000 years ago: Ancestors of the Torres Strait Islanders probably crossed between Australia and Papua New Guinea when the sea level was much lower than today.

1869: People from Tudu Island showed visiting traders where large numbers of pearl shells could be found. This was the beginning of the pearl shell industry in the Torres Strait Islands.

July 1871: The London Missionary Society arrived in the islands and encouraged the local people to become Christians. Torres Strait Islanders celebrate this day as an annual holiday called 'The Coming of the Light'.

1879: Britain claimed the Torres Strait Islands as part of the colony of Queensland.

Aboriginal Nations in Queensland

There are many different Aboriginal nations, each with its own lands and cultural traditions. A nation is defined by its connection to its land and by its language. Groups within a nation may also have their own dialects.

FAST FACTS

Some of the many Aboriginal language groups

Turrbal, Jagerra	Brisbane
Yugambeh	Logan River
Kombumerri, Ngarahngwal	Gold Coast
Jandai, Jandewal, Nunukul, Moondjan, Ngugi, Guwar	Moreton Bay
Kabi Kabi, Joondaburri	Sunshine Coast

European Settlers and the Aboriginal Nations

The Aboriginal nations had strong relationships with the land, and this caused conflict between them and the European settlers. Cattle and sheep replaced native food animals on the land, and settlers colonised areas for themselves that had been in traditional ownership for thousands of years.

WORD FILE

colonise - to settle in a new land and impose a new culture on the people living there
traditional ownership - the Aboriginal land ownership system in existence before the arrival of Europeans
dialects - different forms of the one language
archaeologists - people who study items from the past in human history

Colonial History of Queensland

Up until 1869, Queensland was part of the colony of New South Wales.

Colonial History Timeline

1770	Captain James Cook named Moreton Bay.
1788	The east coast of Australia, including Queensland, is claimed by Britain as the colony of New South Wales.
1823	The Governor in Sydney sent John Oxley to explore land to the north. He found the Brisbane River.
1824	A very harsh convict settlement was built at Moreton Bay, which is now the site of Brisbane.
1842	Free settlers were encouraged to buy land at Moreton Bay.
1859	Queensland became a separate colony.
1860	The new parliament, which originally had two houses, sat for the first time.
1867	Gold was discovered at Gympie.
1901	Federation makes the colony of Queensland a state.

Miners working in a gold mine at Gympie, Queensland

Ludwig Leichhardt

Stamp printed in Australia, shows Ludwig Leichhardt.

Leichhardt was an explorer who was a celebrity of his time. Crowds farewelled him on his expeditions and people waited eagerly to find out what he would discover. The local paper reported that, *'His portrait adorns the window of every shop'*.

In 1844, he travelled from Jimbour in the Darling Downs in Queensland across to the Northern Territory.

Four years later, Leichhardt left Moreton Bay hoping to travel across the country to the Swan River settlement in Western Australia. He disappeared on this journey and no trace of what happened to him has ever been found.

TIME TRAVELLER

Imagine you are leaving with Ludwig Leichhardt to explore the unknown wilderness in the 1840s.
How would you feel?
What are three things you would keep in your pockets at all times and why?

First Newspaper

The Moreton Bay Courier was the first newspaper produced in Queensland. Dating from 1846, it contains fascinating details on the daily lives of the settlers. In the first issue a local shopkeeper advertised a range of goods which had just arrived by ship. They included soap, vinegar, raisins and 'Fancy vests'.

One of the old morse key telegraph machines

First Electric Telegraph

Before the introduction of telephones, the only way settlers communicated with each other over long distances was by letter. These had to be carried by ship, by horse-drawn carriage or by riders on horseback.

The development of the electric telegraph enabled Queenslanders to send messages to each other much more quickly. The first message in Queensland was sent between the mayors of Brisbane and Ipswich in 1861. Messages were sent by Morse Code and written out by hand before being delivered to the person they were addressed to.

FAST FACTS

'Terra Australis' was the European name for Australia before it became a British colony in 1788

Settlers' Houses and Government Buildings

The settlers lived in many different types of housing, depending on how wealthy they were and whether they had convicts or other labourers to help build their houses.

Bark huts - A wooden frame covered in sheets of bark.
Wattle and Daub - A wooden frame plastered with a mixture of clay, straw and manure.
Stone - Government buildings in Moreton Bay, such as the convict barracks, were built from stone or from bricks and timber. The storehouse was built of stone with thick walls to prevent theft. Tools, seeds and food were stored inside the building.
Bricks - Some bricks were brought from England but in 1826 convicts also started making local bricks.

Timber settlers' hut at Aramara Queensland 1896

Transport in Queensland

Pre-Colonial Transport

The first methods of transport used by Aboriginal people in Australia were walking and paddling canoes. Canoes were made of bark or from hollowed out logs, and they were used for fishing and to cross rivers and harbours. 'Canoe trees', which have large scars where bark was peeled from them, occur all across Queensland, near rivers and the coast. There are about 1,500 of these trees around Weipa on Cape York.

Fishing in a bark canoe

A stamp printed in Australia shows a Cobb & Co. Coach (from etching by Sir Lionel Lindsay).

Horses and Coaches

The first settlers walked everywhere, rode horses or travelled in carriages if they could afford them. From 1866 -1924, Cobb & Co coaches pulled by horses were a popular way to go on long journeys in Queensland. The first route was between Brisbane and Toowoomba. Finding food and water for the horses on the long coach journeys was often a problem, and if the ground was very muddy the passengers would have to get out and help push the coach.

Trains

Railways made the transport of produce fast and simple, and they contributed to the economic development of the state. Without railroads, Queensland's coal mining and resources industries would not have developed at the pace they did.

The first railway line in the state opened in 1865 and ran from Ipswich to Grandchester. Queensland's railway lines were often built from a sea port to an inland destination, rather than radiating outwards from Brisbane. Cairns was not linked by rail to Brisbane until the 1920s.

TIME TRAVELLER

Imagine you are on a Cobb & Co coach in the rain and it becomes bogged in the mud.

- **What are you thinking?**
- **How is this different from journeys today?**

During the Second World War, the Queensland railways were vital for transporting ammunition and food as close as possible to the battle zones to the north of Australia.

The sugar train railways are a separate system running on narrow tracks. They support the sugarcane industry, taking the cane to the mills. They first ran in 1866.

Nash's Gully trestle bridge on the Maryborough railway line was part of the railway construction in Queensland during the 1880s

River Transport

As new suburbs grew around Brisbane, many people chose ferries on the river as the easiest way to get to the city. Before the Victoria Bridge was built in 1865, a ferry operated between north and south Brisbane.

Passengers posing on a ferry at the Edward Street ferry terminal, Brisbane, 1890

FAST FACTS

The Dickabram Bridge over the Mary River was built in 1886. It is the oldest large steel truss bridge in Queensland. The name is an Aboriginal word meaning 'sweet potato'.

Shipping Ports

The principal shipping ports today are at Gladstone, Brisbane and Townsville. During the Second World War, Townsville was an important army base and seaport. Warships leaving from Townsville engaged in battles in the Pacific region and also supplied food and equipment to soldiers fighting on land.

The History of Qantas

Qantas was formed in Brisbane in 1920. The letters of the name stand for 'Queensland and Northern Territory Aerial Services Ltd'. The Qantas offices were originally in Winton and then moved to Longreach in 1921. Australia's national airline began flying with only two bi-planes in its fleet. Passengers had to wear helmets and goggles. In the following years, Qantas founded Australia's first flying school. The airline's first overseas passenger flight was between Brisbane and Singapore in 1935.

Boarding an early Qantas aeroplane, 1920-1930

Industry and Mining in Queensland

Queensland mines produce lead, zinc, bauxite and silver and the state is one of the largest exporters of coal in the world. Mining and energy resources make up over 70% of all the state's exports.

Ancient Mining

An Aboriginal stone axe quarry, worked by the Kalkadoon people, has been found by archaeologists at Lake Moondarra near Mount Isa. The axe-heads they made were very hard and were traded with other groups across the northern part of the country. Ochre, or iron oxide, was also mined by Aboriginal people, who used it to create art on rock and cave walls, and for ceremonial body decoration.

Coal Mining

Coal mining is Queensland's highest earning export industry, and it is the source of about 48% of all the coal exported from Australia. There are 32 billion tonnes of coal reserves in Queensland, and 80% of the coal exports go to countries in Asia.

Aluminium Mining

Aluminium comes from a red ore called bauxite and Weipa, on Cape York, has one of the world's largest deposits. Queensland produces 10% of the world's aluminium.

Ore ship loading bauxite at Weipa Queensland

Natural Gas

Natural gas from Queensland provides 20% of gas used in Queensland homes, and exports are expected to bring $15 billion into the state's economy in coming years. Before being exported, gas is turned into a liquid, called LNG, and then transported in specially built tanker ships.

FAST FACTS

SOME OF THE MINING TOWNS IN QUEENSLAND:

- Mount Isa
- Moranbah
- Weipa
- Middlemount
- Emerald
- Clermont
- Dysart

Mount Isa

Mount Isa is an example of a Queensland town which depends on mining for its growth and existence. Located in the Gulf Country in the north of the state, Mount Isa's climate is hot and dry. In 1923, John Miles was looking for areas where he could stake a mining claim. He found copper, silver and zinc deposits and named his claim Mount Isa. The massive deposits of minerals in the area have attracted mining workers for nearly a century, and today Mount Isa Mines is one of the biggest mining operations in Australia.

Lake Moondarra from lookout above Transport Bay near Mount Isa

Aviation

Queensland has nearly 30% of Australia's aviation related businesses, partly as a result of being the state where Qantas was founded. The businesses include maintenance, manufacturing, software and training.

Electricity Industry

There are four sectors in Queensland's electricity industry. They are electricity generation, transmission, distribution and retail. There is a mixture of government and private ownership of these sectors. Most of the electricity is produced using power from burning Queensland coal. The 'Solar 60' program aims to encourage the development of solar power as a renewable energy source.

Tourism

Income from tourists makes up a substantial part of the Queensland economy. Tourists come from interstate as well as from other countries, including New Zealand, the UK, the United States, Europe, China and Japan. Over 20 million visitors arrive every year.

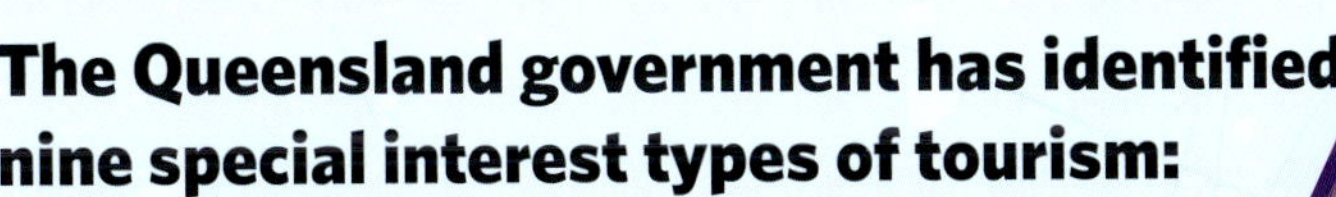

The Queensland government has identified nine special interest types of tourism:

- Backpackers
- Ecotourism
- Indigenous tourism
- Luxury lodges
- Cruise ships
- Food and wine tourism
- International students
- Sports and events
- Self-drive holidays

FUN ACTIVITY

Design your own tourist brochure to encourage people to come to Queensland. Include pictures of the most interesting places you think they would like to visit.

Service Industries

Half of the employment in Brisbane depends on the service industries, which include construction services, education, government, health and retail. Services provided to businesses account for a quarter of the whole Brisbane economy. As large-scale manufacturing decreases in the state, due to much of this work now being done overseas, the service industries are expected to become more important to the financial welfare of Queenslanders.

WORD FILE

service industries - businesses that assist customers rather than making things

Agriculture in Queensland

Agriculture contributes more than $10 billion to Queensland's economy each year. Beef and sugar are two of the largest exports from Queensland's agricultural industry.

Botanic Gardens

The City Botanic Gardens in Brisbane are enjoyed today as a park in the centre of the city, but this area once had a vital role in feeding the colony. Convict gardeners worked there from 1825 to grow the seeds and plants that kept the convicts and settlers from starving. The wheat, sugar and grape growing industries in Queensland were all first trialled in the botanic gardens, where expert gardeners worked out the best way to grow these food crops in the local climate.

Agricultural Products

Fruit, Nuts and Vegetables

Queensland's farmers select plant varieties and growing methods that best suit their environment. In areas where drought is a threat, farmers have to consider the water availability before they plant any crops. Because of its tropical climate, Queensland is a source for many exotic fruits.

Sugarcane

Queensland produces about 95% of Australia's sugar and most of this is exported. This one crop supports many regional towns by providing employment and making use of local businesses. Many sugarcane growers use trickle irrigation, which uses less water than surface irrigation.

QUICK QUIZ

What crop, plant or animal is grown by farmers so that we can have these things in our homes?

- Icing on cakes
- Woollen scarf
- Sausage roll
- Cheese on toast
- Wooden verandah

Cotton

Cotton is grown in the Darling Downs and St George areas, and a large part of it is exported to China. Most of the cotton grown is genetically modified to be resistant to attack by caterpillars.

Wheat

Wheat is grown in southern and central Queensland and is very dependent on the climate. In years of severe drought there may be no wheat grown at all in some areas.

Timber

Queensland has one third of the native forests of Australia. Some of these are logged for timber, but plantations also supply a large part of the timber logged in the state. Building is the main market for this timber, but Queensland needs to import some wood and wood products to meet all its needs. The timber industry contributes about $3.8 billion to Queensland's economy and employs about 19,000 people.

Dairy Farming

Milk production from cows in Queensland is about 7% of the total for Australia. Dairy farms are mostly located in the south-east of the state where the rainfall is high and the climate more temperate.

Beef

Queensland is responsible for about 43% of Australia's total beef exports. Beef cattle are raised in the north and west of the state. Being free from diseases such as foot-and-mouth makes Queensland beef a safe choice for buyers overseas.

Sheep Farming

Sheep are farmed for wool and for their meat. This industry has existed in Queensland since the 1840s. Farmers need to control the feral dogs, foxes and wild pigs that prey on lambs.

Fishing

Commercial fishing operates along the whole coast of Queensland. The different types of fishing methods include trawling, netting, using lines and traps. All commercial fishing is monitored by the government to ensure that areas are not overfished and fish species are preserved.

Biosecurity

Biosecurity is the control of pests and diseases, as well as threats to the environment from dangerous chemicals. Queensland has a number of regulations that control its biosecurity. For example, you cannot bring bananas into the state from certain areas because they may have pests that could destroy local crops.

WHAT CAN YOU DO?

Three things you can do about biosecurity in Queensland

- Don't pour detergents or chemicals into rivers
- Don't bring diseased fruit into farming areas
- Don't release aquarium fish into rivers

Can you think of anything else you could do?

WORD FILE

trickle irrigation - watering crops through tubes laid underground
genetically modified - having genes altered by scientists
trawling - fishing with a large net that drags along the sea floor

Environment and Sustainability in Queensland

Sustainable practices for agriculture and industry require a balance between using the land and waterways for development and keeping areas as regions of natural beauty. The protection of endangered plants and animals is also important.

Bush Fires

Queensland Fire and Emergency Services includes Rural Fire Service volunteers, State Emergency Service volunteers and more than 2,000 permanent firefighters.

Rural Fire Service volunteers provide fire control services in their local area, including:
- fighting fires
- fire prevention, such as controlled burns
- community education
- disaster management response and recovery operations

RESOURCES	HOW WE CAN LOOK AFTER THEM
SOIL	Correct use of fertilisers and avoiding soil erosion
FORESTS	Using plantations for timber
WATER	Keeping water supplies unpolluted
NATIVE PLANTS	Avoid complete clearing of areas for pastures
NATIVE ANIMALS	Keep some areas of natural bushland for food and shelter
AIR QUALITY	Avoid polluting the air through poor industrial practices

Protecting Native Plants & Animals

Endangered animals in Queensland are affected by habitat loss, introduced species, infectious diseases, fire and climate change. Some of these animals are:
- Grey nurse shark
- Greater bilby
- Northern hairy nosed wombat
- Proserpine rock wallaby
- Leatherback turtle

National Parks

Queensland manages its national parks so they remain in their natural state as much as possible. Pest plants and animals are destroyed or removed. They include foxes and feral goats, dogs and pigs. Visitors are asked to clean their vehicles before entering a national park, to stop them bringing in weeds, insect pests or diseases that might affect the wildlife.

Marine Parks

Marine parks protect many habitats, including mangroves, seagrass beds, mudflats, sandbanks, beaches, rocky outcrops and reefs.

Energy Production

About 81% of Queensland's electricity is generated by coal-fired power stations. Research into low emission coal technology is looking for ways to make coal a cleaner energy source. Research is also being done on producing energy from renewable sources such as

- biofuel production (ethanol and biodiesel)
- next generation organic solar cells
- geothermal energy

Coastal Erosion

The Queensland government encourages people in coastal areas to plan for high tides, erosion by the sea and the effects of rising sea levels.

Water Use

Licences are required to drill a bore hole for water or for using water from rivers for industry and agriculture. The Great Artesian Basin, which is the largest in the world, is an underground source of water which lies beneath most of Queensland. It provides a water source for people living and farming in the driest areas of the state.

Extreme Weather

Floods, drought and tropical cyclones are a threat to property, industry and wildlife. There have been over 200 cyclones on the east coast since 1858. Drought and floods destroy crops and grazing areas and drown livestock. The first recorded great flood on the Brisbane River was in1841. Since then, floods have often damaged Brisbane's homes and businesses.

The Queensland government has a variety of emergency measures in place to respond to extreme weather events and to protect life and property. Some scientists say that climate change is causing Queensland to experience more extreme weather events than in the past.

The Cane Toad

The cane toad is an introduced species. Originally released into the sugarcane fields in 1935 to control the beetles that were eating the crop, the cane toad began killing native wildlife. It has been responsible for poisoning pets and is a threat to people as well. The cane toad is gradually making its way beyond Queensland's state borders, and it threatens the sanctuary of Kakadu in the Northern Territory.

WORD FILE

sustainability - ability of the environment to be used without being destroyed
plantations - farms used to grow one product, such as trees for timber

PESKY PESTS

Yellow Crazy Ant
Cane Toad
Crown of Thorns Starfish
Prickly Pear

The Great Barrier Reef

This World Heritage Site is a magnificent coral reef that extends along a large part of Queensland's coast. The reef provides habitats for an immense range of marine animals and plants.

Aboriginal History

Many Aboriginal nations lived along the coast beside the Great Barrier Reef and travelled back and forth between its islands. They fished the waters, hunted turtles and gathered shellfish. There have been many archaeological finds along the coast, including evidence of the lifestyle of the Darumbal people who lived around the Rockhampton area. They left shell middens, stone arrangements and scarred trees. Bark from these trees was used to build canoes.

Colonial History

Captain James Cook's ship, The Endeavour, was damaged on the reef in 1770. He mapped the area and found Cook's Passage, which is one of the few safe passages between the open sea and the mainland.

HMS Endeavour, Thomas Luny

Great Barrier Reef Marine Park

In 1975, the reef became a Marine Park with different types of environmental protection depending on the zoning.
The zones are:

- General Use
- Habitat Protection
- Conservation Park
- Marine National Park
- Preservation

Permitted activities in the zones range from limited boating and fishing in the General Use Zone to entry by permit for research only in the Preservation Zone. Large ships must use special shipping lanes.

FAST FACTS

The Great Barrier Reef is 2,300 km long and is the largest living structure on earth.

EXPLORE IT YOURSELF

Use Google Maps to find the Great Barrier Reef. What are three things you can see about it that are different from the mainland nearby?

Threats to the Great Barrier Reef

Crown Of Thorns Starfish

This pest starfish destroys the coral by eating it. There are a number of programs underway to control the Crown of Thorns without introducing dangerous chemicals that would also kill the other marine animals.

Development

Ports, tourist sites and towns along the coast have buildings and pollutants that can affect the reef by destroying natural coastal ecosystems.

Climate Change

Coral bleaching occurs when coral dies. A rise in the water temperature due to climate change can cause this.

Tourism

Tourists need accommodation and like to explore the reef and see its wildlife. These activities can place stress on the reef and its water quality.

Agriculture

Run-off from agricultural land on the mainland can enter rivers and then end up on the reef. This water may be carrying pesticides and fertilisers which will damage the marine ecosystems.

Litter Control

Litter can be deposited in the reef by rivers and from boats. Plastic litter is particularly damaging since it does not degrade.

Extreme Weather

Floods on the mainland send water down rivers and into the reef area. This water reduces the salinity of the reef and it also contains silt and pollutants which can kill coral. Cyclones cause structural damage to the reef.

Government of Queensland

Queensland is the only state of Australia to have a unicameral parliament.

Timeline Before Federation

UP TO 1788 Australian Aboriginal nations governed according to their own laws.

1770 Captain James Cook explored the coast of eastern Australia and claimed the land for Britain.

1788 Governor Phillip was the highest authority in the colony.

1859 Brisbane had the first local government in the state.

1859 Queensland became a separate colony.

1860 The new parliament, which had two houses, sat for the first time.

Early view from Bowen Terrace towards Parliament House.

FAST FACTS

'Terra nullius' is Latin meaning 'land that nobody owns'. The British government used this idea to allow them to claim land in Queensland.

FAST FACTS

The imprisonment of strikers after the shearers' strike at Barcaldine in 1891 was one of the events leading to the formation of the Australian Labor Party.

Commonwealth Procession. Brisbane 1.1.01.
A.N.A. Display.

Timeline After Federation

1901 Federation meant the colony of Queensland became a separate state.

1905 Women could vote in Queensland.

1915 Women could stand for election to parliament in Queensland.

1921 Queensland abolishes its upper house of parliament.

1965 Aboriginal Queenslanders could vote in state and federal elections.

1973 People over the age of 18 could vote.

Local Government

Queensland has 77 local government councils. They look after local services such as suburban streets, libraries, garbage collection and parks. The first local government council created in Queensland was for Brisbane in1859, followed by Ipswich, Ioowoomba and Rockhampton.

The Queensland Parliament Today

There is only one section, or house, in the Queensland parliament. This is the Legislative Assembly and it has 89 members. All members are elected by voters. The Legislative Council, or Upper House, was abolished in 1921, resulting in Queensland having a unicameral system of government.

WORD FILE

unicameral - a government having only one house or section

Notable People from Queensland

Government and Politics

Eddie Mabo (1936 - 1992) was born on Murray (Mer) Island in the Torres Strait. He took his claims for traditional land ownership rights on Murray Island to the High Court of Australia and won. This success encouraged other claims for land rights by Aboriginal Australians across the nation.

Quentin Bryce (1942 -) was born in Brisbane. She was the Governor General of Australia from 2008 to 2014, and was the first woman to hold this position.

Sport

Cathy Freeman (1973 -) was born in Mackay. Her gold medal in the 400 metre sprint in the 2000 Olympic Games in Sydney was celebrated by the whole country. Cathy was also the first Aboriginal Australian to win a gold medal at the Commonwealth Games.

Greg Norman (1955 -) was born in Mount Isa. He is a world renowned golfer who was ranked number one for 331 weeks. Nicknamed 'The Shark' because of his aggressive golfing style.

Rod Laver (1938 -) was born in Rockhampton. One of Australia's greatest tennis players, he was world number one from 1964 - 1970.

Poetry

Oodgeroo Noonuccal, also known as Kath Walker, (1920 - 1993) was born on North Stradbroke Island. Her poetry explores the land and the intense relationship that Aboriginal Australians have with nature.

MAKE YOUR OWN LIST

Who are three people you think are important in your family, school or suburb?

What makes a person memorable?

Conservation

Bindi Irwin (1991 -) was born in Buderim in 1998. She is the daughter of Steve Irwin and continues his work caring for wildlife and being active in conservation. Her popular series of children's stories encourages young people to think about the plight of endangered animals. Bindi is also an actress and star of a television series in which she entertained viewers with stories about animals around the world.

Sailing

Jessica Watson (1993 -) was born on the Gold Coast. In 2010, at only 16 years old, she became the youngest person ever to sail around the world solo. In 2011, she was the Young Australian of the Year.

Aviation

Charles Kingsford Smith (1897 - 1935) was born in Brisbane. In 1928, he succeeded in becoming the first person to fly across the Pacific Ocean from the United States to Australia. His plane, named the Southern Cross, was greeted by 25,000 people when it finally arrived in Brisbane.

Bert Hinkler (1892 - 1933) was born in Bundaberg. In 1928, he made the first solo flight from Britain to Australia.

Education

Dorothy Hill (1907 - 1997) was born in Brisbane. She was Australia's first female university professor, and the first female president of the Australian Academy of Science. As a geologist she undertook pioneering research into the Great Barrier Reef.

Dramatic Arts

Geoffrey Rush (1951 -) was born in Toowoomba. He has won numerous international awards for his stage and screen performances. His best known films are The King's Speech, Shine and Pirates of the Caribbean. In 2012, he was named Australian of the Year.

Immigration to Queensland

People have come from around the world to live and work in Queensland. Their cultures and skills have contributed to the social diversity of the state.

60,000 Years Ago

At least 50,000 years ago, the ancestors of the Australian Aboriginal people arrived from the north and spread throughout the country. The northern parts of Queensland were joined to the landmass of Papua New Guinea 8,000 years ago, when the sea levels were much lower than they are today, and people could travel easily across the shallow seas.

The Kanakas

Queensland did not have the benefit of a large convict population to provide the low cost labour needed to build the early economy. Workers for the sugarcane industry had to be found elsewhere and some people looked to the islands of the South Pacific to supply them. The founder of Townsville, Robert Towns, decided to import people to work in the sugarcane plantations. They mostly came from Vanuatu and the Solomon Islands as well as various other Pacific Islands. Lured onto ships, they were brought to Queensland, where they were treated much like slaves and not allowed to leave. The islanders became known as Kanakas. Between 1863 and 1904, 62,000 South Sea Islanders were brought to Australia.

South Sea Islanders working in the canefields in North Queensland

Portrait of two South Sea Islanders from the Pioneer Sugar Mill, Brandon, Queensland, 1880s

General Douglas MacArthur and aide

World War II

The Second World War came very close to Queensland's northern border when the Japanese invaded Papua New Guinea. Large numbers of soldiers from the United States and Australia were sent to Queensland so they could be ready for battle. In 1942, Brisbane's population doubled due to the influx of troops. The Allied commander for the Pacific, General Douglas MacArthur, had his headquarters in Brisbane during the Second World War.

FAST FACTS

In 1942, during WWII, Townsville's population grew from 30,000 to nearly 100,000 due to the large number of troops stationed there.

What Countries Have They Come From?

Today, migrants to Queensland arrive mainly from Britain, New Zealand, South Africa, China and India. Most of the recent migrants have chosen to live in the large population centres of Brisbane, Gold Coast, Sunshine Coast, Logan and Cairns. Queensland has also recently welcomed people from Afghanistan, Iraq and Somalia.

Emigration in search of a husband, 1833

Great Britain

Between 1860 and 1901, 250,000 people were encouraged to migrate to Queensland from Britain. Because the ships carrying them came from the north, Queensland became the only state to have immigrants settle in a number of small towns along its coast, rather than all mostly going straight to the capital city. Cairns, Townsville and Rockhampton were settled in this way.

German settler and his family, Rosewood Scrub, ca. 1880

Germany

The colonial government sent an agent to Germany to encourage people there to migrate. About 13% of the early migrants came from Germany. German place names and Lutheran churches show where they settled.

Scandinavia

The countries of Sweden, Denmark, Norway and Finland were also targeted by the colonial Queensland government in its search for more migrants to fill the local demand for labour. Posters and pamphlets stressed the warm climate and opportunities that migrants would find when they arrived.

Italy

In the early 1900s, Italian migrants were encouraged to migrate to Queensland to work in the sugarcane industry. Many eventually bought farms for themselves and prospered.

China

Chinese were originally welcomed to ease the labour shortage in colonial Queensland. They came in large numbers to the Palmer River goldfield and also helped to build the sugarcane and banana growing industries.

DID YOU KNOW?

Migrants to Queensland have come from many other countries apart from the ones listed above. How many can you name?

Afghanistan

Colonial Queensland depended on Afghani migrants and their camels to deliver goods to remote areas which had hot, dry climates. Although they were all called Afghans by Queenslanders, the cameleers also came from a number of other Middle Eastern countries.

Major Sites in Queensland

These sites include buildings, structures and natural features. They are important for their beauty, rarity and history.

FAST FACTS

World Heritage Sites in Queensland:

1. Fraser Island
2. Gondwana Rainforests of Australia
3. Great Barrier Reef
4. Riversleigh
5. The Wet Tropics

Gondwana Rainforests

These sub-tropical rainforests are located in the southeast of Queensland. The Lamington National Park is a part of these forests. The plants found here are direct descendants of the vegetation that once grew on the ancient continent of Gondwana.

Great Barrier Reef

The world's most diverse coral reef. It extends along a large part of the coast of Queensland.

The Gold Coast

The Gold Coast attracts tourists from around the world. It is famous for its beautiful beaches, including Surfers Paradise.

Fraser Island

Fraser Island is the world's largest sand island. It is 123 kilometres long and 25 kilometres wide.

Australian Stockman's Hall of Fame

Opened by Queen Elizabeth in 1988 at Longreach, this museum explores the life and work of the outback stockman in Queensland's history.

Riversleigh

Riversleigh is in the Boodjamulla (Lawn Hill) National Park. It has the richest known fossil mammal deposits in Australia. Searches there have revealed fossils from the ancient Gondwanan continent. The site is very remote, and some areas have restricted access.

Wet Tropics and the Daintree Rainforest

The Daintree Rainforest, which is a wet tropical system, is important because its range of plants is representative of most of the stages of plant evolution on earth. It is a growing museum.

Old Government House

Old Government House in Brisbane was completed in 1862 and Queensland governors lived there until 1909. All the sandstone used to build it had to be floated down the river on punts from Goodna. Old Government House is now a museum and function venue.

Gold Coast Theme Parks

The theme parks on the Gold Coast attract tourists from around Australia and the world. As well as providing enjoyment for so many people, the theme parks contribute to Queensland's economy and to employment in the region.

Flags, Symbols, Emblems and Special Days of Queensland

People living in Queensland use flags, symbols and special days to show their connection to their community. These connections include pride for the group they belong to, an interest in the history of their group or area, and wanting to join others for celebrations that bring people together.

Queensland State Flag

The Queensland flag was first used in 1876. The Union Jack is a reminder of the ties with Britain. The crown represents Queen Victoria, who reigned when the flag was designed. The origin of the use of the blue Maltese Cross may be a reference to the Victoria Cross, but the real reason for its use has never been recorded.

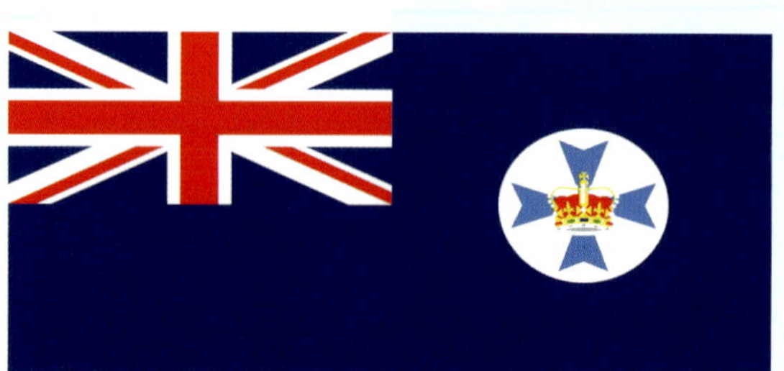

Australian Aboriginal Flag

The Aboriginal flag was first flown in 1971. It was designed by Elder Harold Thomas.

Yellow disc - the sun and yellow ochre
Red - the land
Black - the Aboriginal people of Australia

RULES FOR FLYING THESE FLAGS

- **Don't fly more than one on the same pole.**
- **Don't fly them in the dark.**
- **Raise the flag to the top of the pole before lowering it to half-mast.**
- **Treat these flags with respect.**

The Torres Strait Flag

First flown in 1992 and designed by Bernard Namok.
White Dhari (headdress) - a symbol of the Torres Strait Islanders
White five-pointed star - symbolises peace and the five major island groups
Green stripes - the land
Black stripes- the people
Blue - the sea

Special Days

Australia Day - On 26th January each year, Australians commemorate the founding of a British colony by Governor Phillip at Sydney Cove in 1788.
ANZAC Day - Ceremonies and marches for ANZAC Day are held all around the state on 25th April each year. The largest march in the state is in Brisbane.
NAIDOC Week - A week in July each year to celebrate the history, culture and achievements of Aboriginal and Torres Strait Islander peoples. Various communities and local and Queensland governments organise events around the state for NAIDOC Week.

The Torres Strait Islands have many special days for their history and religion.
Mabo Day, 3rd June - Celebrates Eddie Mabo's land rights victory in the Australian High Court.
Coming of the Light, 1st July - Celebrates the day Christianity was brought to the Torres Strait Islands.

Symbols of Queensland

Floral Emblem - Cooktown orchid
Animal Emblem - Koala
Bird Emblem - Brolga
Fish Emblem - Anemone fish
Gemstone Emblem - Sapphire

The Coat of Arms

This is a symbol of Queensland and each part of it has a meaning.
Crest - represents sugarcane
Red Deer - Queen Victoria gave Queensland a herd of red deer
Brolga - represents the bird emblem
Ram's Head - represents the sheep industry
Bull's Head - represents the cattle industry
Wheat - represents the wheat industry
Quartz - represents the mining industry
Motto - 'Audax at Fidelis" - these Latin words mean 'Bold but Faithful'.

Make Your Own Coat of Arms

Design a Coat of Arms for your family, suburb or sport group, etc.

- Use symbols that everyone will know
- Your own Coat of Arms could include drawings or pictures to tell the history of the group
- Think about where to use your Coat of Arms
- What language will you use for a motto?
- Where have you seen the Queensland Coat of Arms used?

WORD FILE

Elder - a respected Aboriginal person who is a custodian of traditional knowledge
half-mast - flying a flag halfway up the pole as a mark of respect when a community leader dies
motto - a few words that express the ideals of a group

How to Find Out More
Primary and Secondary Sources

There are many ways to find out more about Queensland. You can do this using both primary and secondary sources. Websites can have a mixture of both types of sources on them.

Primary Sources

- **Interviews** - when people say what they have seen
- **Letters** - when the writer was the person experiencing the event
- **Newspapers** - when the facts are presented
- **Photos** - when they have not been altered
- **Maps**
- **Old Items & Antiques**
- **News on Television** - when it shows pictures of real events or a person saying what they have seen
- **School Newsletters** - when they list names or dates of events
- **Videos on Youtube or Facebook** - when they show an event and have not been altered

Secondary Sources

- **Letters** - when the writer is retelling the facts that someone else told them
- **Newspapers** - when the story is told by someone who retells the facts that someone else told them
- **Photos** - when the photo has been altered
- **Songs, Poems, Stories**
- **News on Television** - when it is reported by journalists who did not experience the events

Fun Activities Using Sources

- Find old newspapers at your local library. Use these to look at pictures of areas you know and see how they have changed over time.
- Take photos of your school, paste them into an exercise book, add some notes and ask the librarian to add your book to the collection. This will then become a primary source for students in the future.
- Ask students and teachers to tell you what they know about the history of your school. Type the results into a Word document, print it and staple the pages into a booklet. You now have a secondary source for people to use in the future. Ask the librarian to add your booklet to the library collection.

Museums

Visit your local museum to find primary sources. You could look for examples of clothing that the convict labourers wore and compare it with the uniforms of their guards or the dresses owned by the free women settlers.

- Queensland Museum, Brisbane
- Queensland Maritime Museum, Brisbane
- Australian Stockman's Hall of Fame, Longreach
- Qantas Founders Museum, Longreach
- Museum of Tropical Queensland, Townsville
- Cobb+Co Museum, Toowoomba

Your Own Family and Friends

Primary sources do not always have to be about famous people. Interviews with your family and friends are important too. Your grandmother might recall what your suburb used to be like. Friends can share stories about coming to live in Queensland, either from other states or from a country overseas.

Websites

- Find out all about Queensland at this state government website, www.qld.gov.au/queenslanders
- Search for places in Queensland, www.queenslandplaces.com.au/home
- Queensland Historical Atlas, www.qhatlas.com.au